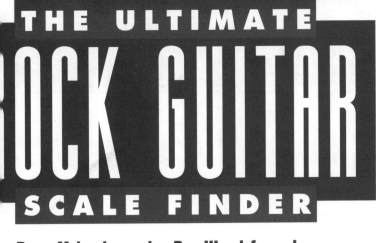

THE ULTIMATE ROCK GUITAR SCALE FINDER

By Michael P. Wolfsohn

ISBN 0-7935-1669-2

HAL•LEONARD®
CORPORATION

7777 W. BLUEMOUND RD. P.O. BOX 13819 MILWAUKEE, WI 53213

Foreword

*T*his book is about scales – about finding them and using them. It begins by telling you how scales relate to chords, and then shows you all the important scales used in rock, where they are and how to use them.

There is a lot of information in this book, and there are several ways to use it. Taking the time to go through it once from the beginning will help you see very quickly how it is organized, and how it will be of the most use to you.

Be a little patient with yourself — this is one of the areas of music that can seem like pure Greek until suddenly something clicks and you say "Oh, yeah, of course, I get it!!!!" Going over the same material repeatedly can bring you to that moment of insight much sooner.

How To Use This book

*Y*ou may use this book in three different ways:

- **As a dictionary of scale forms**

  When you need to find the "shape" of a scale — it's relative fret placements and fingering, look it up in the appropriate scale section, and then use the Theory section to find the correct location on the fretboard.

- **As a guide to scale/chord relationships**

  When you need to understand how a scale relates to a set of chords, look in the theory sections for explanations.

- **As a source of harmonic ideas**

  When you want to find new sounds, try out some of the different scales with their respective chords to expand your musical horizons.

Chord/Scale Relations

Chords and scales are intimately related — chords are derived from scales. In this chapter, we will look at how chords are formed from scales, the relationship between chords and scales, and how to use this information to find the right scale for a set of chords.

Here is a *C major* scale in tablature, with the half-steps and whole-steps between the notes shown. (If you don't know what half-steps and whole-steps are, try consulting a music theory book such as *Guitar Techniques - Music Theory for Guitar* published by the Hal Leonard Corporation.

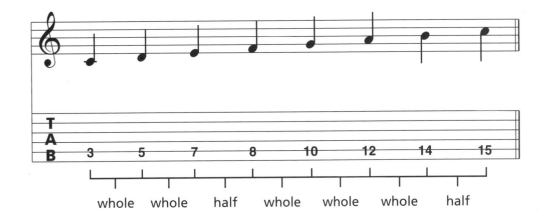

Now, here is the same scale as *diatonic triads* with the intervals shown. Each of these triads consists of a scale tone from the *C major* scale as the root (or name tone) and two more notes that form intervals of a third and of a fifth relative to the root. (Again, if you don't know what roots, intervals, thirds, fifths, etc. are, try consulting a music theory book.) The type of third or fifth that occur in each chord will vary — only notes from the scale are used to form diatonic triads, and whatever type of interval occurs is used.

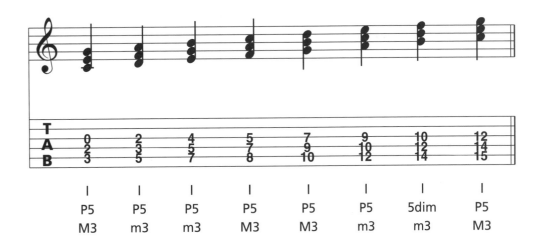

Here are the diatonic triads again, this time with the type of chord shown:

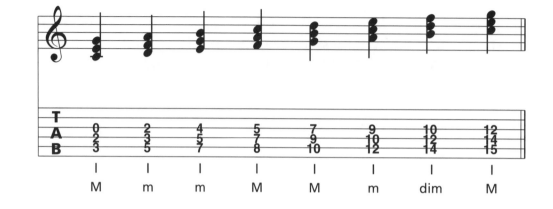

Notice the sequence — **major, minor, minor, major, major, minor, diminished**. This sequence will occur in every major scale, no matter which note you start on. Therefore, these triads can be referred to by number. (In this book, roman numerals are used for diatonic chords — upper case numerals are used for major chords, lower case for minor chords.)

Here is the scale again, with the numbered chords shown.

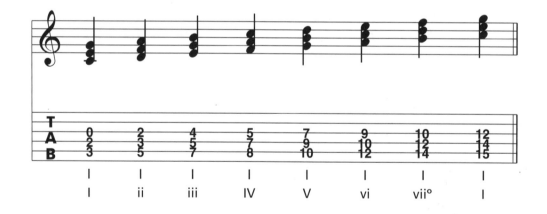

It is important to know both the color of the chord (major, minor, etc..), it's position in the scale (I, ii, etc.) and the half-step/whole-step relationships between the scale steps (whole-whole-half, etc.) to be able to find the appropriate scale or scales to use with a group of chords.

Diatonic seventh chords can be derived in the same way that diatonic triads are — by building chords consisting of a root, third, fifth and seventh on each step of a scale using only notes in the scale. Here are diatonic sevenths for the *C major* scale.

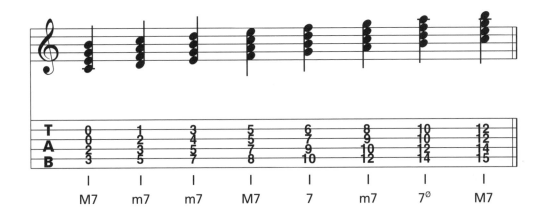

The most important of these is the one that falls on the fifth step of the scale. This is called a dominant-type seventh (the fifth step of a major scale is called the dominant). The only place that this type of seventh is found in the major scale system is on the fifth step. This is an extremely important piece of information — so important that we will include it even when looking at triads.

Here, finally, is the *C major* scale as diatonic triads, with the possibility of a dominant-type seventh on the fifth step indicated).

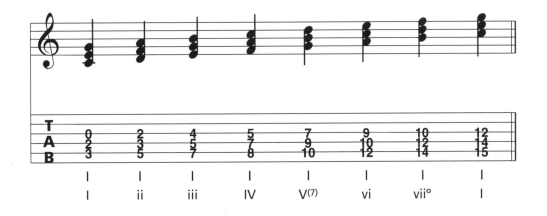

Later, we will use this information to find scales for chord progressions in major, minor and modal keys. First, though, we need to look at blues and blues/rock scales and chords.

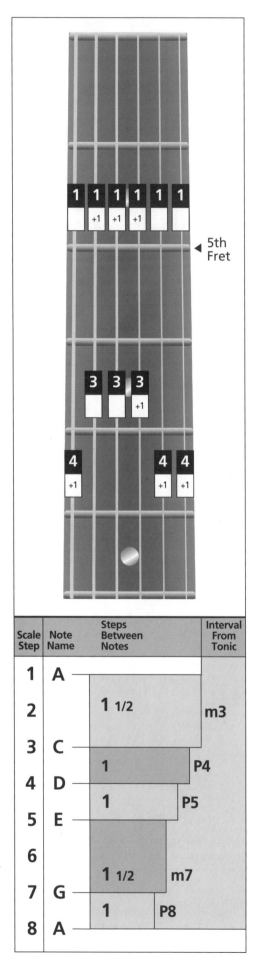

Scale Step	Note Name	Steps Between Notes	Interval From Tonic
1	A		
2		1 1/2	m3
3	C	1	P4
4	D	1	P5
5	E		
6		1 1/2	m7
7	G	1	P8
8	A		

*I*n the next several sections (the sections discussing the various scales) you will encounter two types of charts — a "Shape" chart, such as the one to the left, and a "Steps/Intervals" chart, such as the one below the "Shape" chart.

A "Shape" chart is simply a picture of a guitar neck, shown as if the guitar were standing up. The divided rectangles placed on the neck indicate the following:

● The placement of the rectangle indicates a fret that is included in the scale shape being discussed. For example, in the chart on this page, 6th string/5th fret, 6th string/8th fret, 5th string/5th fret, etc. are all included. The important thing to learn is the "shape" of the scale patterns — all of the "shapes" in this book are moveable.

● The large number in the upper half of the rectangle indicates left-hand fingering. For example, in the chart on this page, 6th string/5th fret is played with the 1st (or index) finger of the fret hand.

● The smaller number(s) in the lower half of the rectangle indicate how far (if at all) the note may be bent (up to a whole step — larger bends are not being considered in this book). For example, in the chart on this page, 4th string/7th fret (played with the 3rd or ring finger) may be bent a whole step.

A "Steps/Intervals" chart gives you additional information about the scale. Starting with the left column:

● It tells you which scale steps are included (as compared to a major scale, which contains seven notes and then repeats an octave higher). Chromatically altered notes (sharps and flats) are shown in between the unaltered scale steps.

● It tells you the letter names of all the notes.

● It tells you how many steps there are between consecutive notes.

● It tells you the interval from the root (tonic, or first note) of the scale to each of the other notes in the scale.

Blues/Rock Scales

Blues has colored and affected rock more than any other musical style. A lot of early rock 'n' roll is basically blues with new rhythms. As rock 'n' roll developed into rock, it took its blues roots with it. Many major pioneer and contemporary rock artists, from Jimi Hendrix and Eric Clapton to Stevie Ray Vaughan, Robert Cray and ZZ Top have made music filled with blues.

Blues is also the easiest place to begin learning to improvise, because you need only stay within the scale — all of the notes work with all of the chords.

The reason for this is that blues is built on an entirely different harmonic idea than major, minor or modal music. There are two important ways in which blues differs:

- **All** of the chords in a Blues harmonic setting are (or can be) dominant-type seventh chords. (You will recall from the last chapter that in a major key only **one** chord can be a dominant-type seventh. It is also true in minor and modal keys that only one chord can be a dominant-type seventh.)

- In major, minor and modal keys, the chords are derived from a scale — that is, they only contain notes found in that scale. In Blues keys, dominant-type seventh chords may be constructed on each step of the scale. These chords may contain notes that are not found in the scale.

Chords may be thought of as **consonant** or **dissonant.** Consonant chords (majors, minors and their substitutes) tend to sound complete when played — there is no implied motion. When a dissonant chord (sevenths and their substitutes) is played, however, there is an immediate sense of tension, and a sense that another chord needs to be played to resolve that tension.

For example play the three examples below:

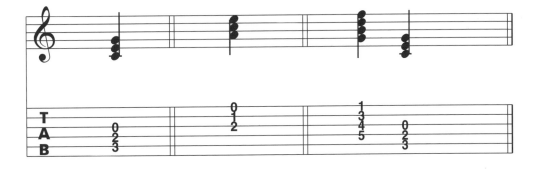

The first two (*C major* and *A minor,* respectively) sound fine as played. The third (*D7*), however, doesn't seem complete until you move to the *A major* chord.

Blues-based music, since it is built on sevenths is inherently dissonant.

Pentatonic Scale

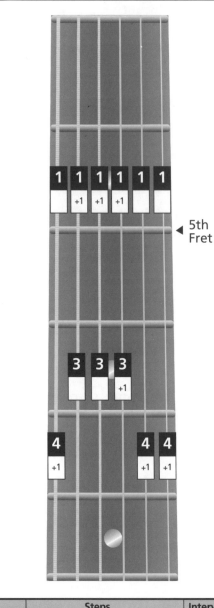

*T*here are two different kinds of pentatonic scales — the minor pentatonic scale and the major pentatonic scale. Each contains five notes (hence the prefix "penta" from the Latin for "five").

Rock music uses both, but because blues and blues-based rock rely heavily upon it, we will begin with the minor pentatonic scale.

Since pentatonic scales contain five notes and all of the major, minor and modal scales contain seven notes, it is important to understand the relationship between the notes in the minor pentatonic scale and those in the other scales.

As a point of reference, we will examine several things in each scale that we explore:

- the names of the notes in the scale being explored

- the interval from the tonic (or 1st tone) of the scale to each of the subsequent notes).

- the distance between the notes in whole-steps and half-steps

- the preferred fingering for the scale-shape being explored

- the customary half-step and whole-step bends available in the scale being explored

Below is tablature for the *A minor pentatonic* scale: shown in the charts at the left:

Scale Step	Note Name	Steps Between Notes	Interval From Tonic
1	A		
2		1 1/2	m3
3	C		
4	D	1	P4
5	E	1	P5
6			
7	G	1 1/2	m7
8	A	1	P8

Note that as compared to a standard seven-note scale, this scale has no 2nd step and no 6th step. This can also be seen in the fact that there is no interval of a second or a sixth between the tonic and any of the notes in the scale.

This is very useful in two ways:

● the second and sixth degrees define scales, the lack of them leaves a skeleton that can be played in place of many others (more on this as we go along).

● The lack of these steps leaves a "pentatonic shell" to which we can add different seconds and sixths to create complete seven-note scale shapes that are based upon this familiar shape.

Memorize this scale shape. Practice playing it ascending and descending, and practice all the bends. Once you have this shape memorized in the fifth position (as shown here) you are ready to move it around on the fretboard.

Here is a table showing which minor pentatonic scale you are playing at all the positions available on a 22-fret guitar. (Positions 20 and above would be incomplete and are therefore omitted.)

POSITION	SCALE
open	E minor pentatonic
1	F minor pentatonic
2	F#/G♭ minor pentatonic
3	G minor pentatonic
4	G#/A♭ minor pentatonic
5	A minor pentatonic
6	A#/B♭ minor pentatonic
7	B minor pentatonic
8	C minor pentatonic
9	C#/D♭ minor pentatonic
10	D minor pentatonic
11	D#/E♭ minor pentatonic
12	E minor pentatonic
13	F minor pentatonic
14	F#/G♭ minor pentatonic
15	G minor pentatonic
16	G#/A♭ minor pentatonic
17	A minor pentatonic
18	A#/B♭ minor pentatonic
19	B minor pentatonic

Below is a table showing some typical chord progressions for minor pentatonic keys, both for the key of *A minor* and as scale steps. When you encounter these progressions, you can play the appropriate minor pentatonic scale.

Remember, the scale steps are from this scale. (For example, III in this key is a minor third up from the tonic.)

For A Minor	As Scale Steps
Am, Dm, Em	i, iv, v
Am, C, Dm, Em	i, III, iv, v
Am, G	i, VII

Blues Scale

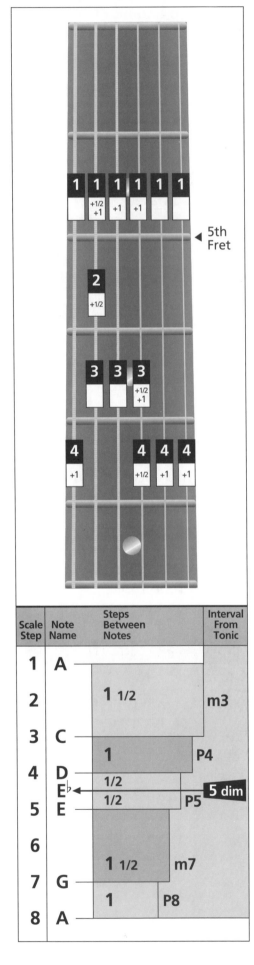

Scale Step	Note Name	Steps Between Notes		Interval From Tonic
1	A			
2		1 1/2		m3
3	C			
		1		P4
4	D			
		1/2		5 dim
	E♭			
		1/2		P5
5	E			
6				
		1 1/2		m7
7	G			
		1		P8
8	A			

The blues scale differs from the minor pentatonic scale in one small but important way — the addition of the flat-fifth note. This scale then contains two different fifths — the perfect fifth and the flat fifth. (major, minor and modal scales never contain more than one type of fifth.)

This note is very dissonant — when you play it, it creates a great deal of tension that wants to be resolved by moving to another note. This is similar to but more pronounced than the tension created by playing the third step of this scale (which is a minor third up from the root) against the dominant-type seventh chord built on the root of the scale which contains the **major** third (which is not found in the scale).

Record yourself playing an *A7* chord (or have a friend play it). While the chord is playing, play these two examples:

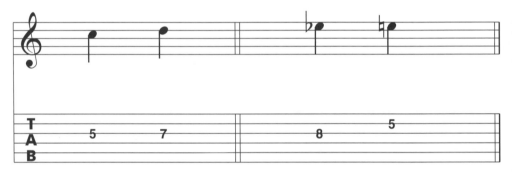

Notice the tension as you play the first note, and the resolution as you move to the second. This is characteristic of blues and blues-based music.

Here is tablature for the *A blues* scale shown in the charts at the left:

Note that as compared to a standard seven-note scale, this scale (like the minor pentatonic) is lacking the 2nd step and the 6th step. This can also be seen in the fact that there is no interval of a second or a sixth between the tonic and any of the notes in the scale.

Notice, too, that the addition of the flat-five note changes the bending options on the fourth step of this scale. You may now bend this note up either a half-step or a whole-step, where, in the minor pentatonic scale, your only option was a whole-step bend.

Memorize this scale shape. Practice playing it ascending and descending, and practice all the bends. Practice switching from the minor pentatonic to the complete blues scale. This is useful in two ways:

● It reinforces both scales. You will use both scales at various times in improvising, as they have somewhat different sounds, and because the minor pentatonic (as you will see) has many other uses besides its use as a partial blues scale.

● It prepares you for more advanced scale-switching later.

Here is a table showing which blues scale you are playing at all the positions available on a 22-fret guitar. (Positions 20 and above would be incomplete and are therefore omitted.)

POSITION	SCALE
open	E blues scale
1	F blues scale
2	F♯/G♭ blues scale
3	G blues scale
4	G♯/A♭ blues scale
5	A blues scale
6	A♯/B♭ blues scale
7	B blues scale
8	C blues scale
9	C♯/D♭ blues scale
10	D blues scale
11	D♯/E♭ blues scale
12	E blues scale
13	F blues scale
14	F♯/G♭ blues scale
15	G blues scale
16	G♯/A♭ blues scale
17	A blues scale
18	A♯/B♭ blues scale
19	B blues scale

Below is a table showing some typical chord progressions for blues keys, both for the key of *A blues* and as scale steps. When you encounter these progressions, you can play the appropriate blues scale.

Remember, the scale steps are from this scale. (For example, III in this key is a minor third up from the tonic.)

For A blues	As Scale Steps
A7, D7, E7	I⁷, IV⁷, V⁷
A, C, D, E	I, III, IV, V
A7, G	I⁷, VII

Major Blues Scale

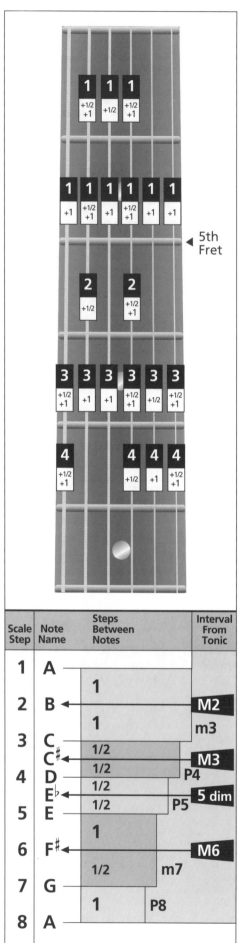

With the addition of three notes from the major scale, the blues scale becomes the major blues scale and takes on a whole new "feel".

The three notes that are added are the major third (in addition to the minor third from the normal blues scale), the major second and the major sixth. All of these notes have a strong major-scale feel to them (especially the major third, which is one of the defining notes in a major chord).

Try playing the following two examples while another guitar or a tape recording plays an *A7* chord:

Notice that the first example (all notes from the normal blues scale) sounds very bluesy and dissonant in spots, while the second example adds some of the "happy" major sound to the basic blues feel. Mastering this scale, then gives you a different "feel" that you can add to your blues soloing arsenal.

Here is tablature for the *A major blues* scale shown in the charts at the left:

Notice that on the 3rd, 4th and 5th strings the index finger may play either of two notes. Frequently you slide from one to the other. For example:

Memorize this scale shape, and practice switching from the normal blue scale to the major blues scale. Many great blues players will use one of these scales in one section of a song and the other in other sections to help vary their sound and make their music more interesting.

Here is a table showing which major blues scale you are playing at all the positions available on a 22-fret guitar. (Positions 20 and above would be incomplete and are therefore omitted.)

POSITION	SCALE
open	E major blues scale
1	F major blues scale
2	F♯/G♭ major blues scale
3	G major blues scale
4	G♯/A♭ major blues scale
5	A major blues scale
6	A♯/B♭ major blues scale
7	B major blues scale
8	C major blues scale
9	C♯/D♭ major blues scale
10	D major blues scale
11	D♯/E♭ major blues scale
12	E major blues scale
13	F major blues scale
14	F♯/G♭ major blues scale
15	G major blues scale
16	G♯/A♭ major blues scale
17	A major blues scale
18	A♯/B♭ major blues scale
19	B major blues scale

Below is a table showing some typical chord progressions for major blues keys, both for the key of *A major blues* and as scale steps. When you encounter these progressions, you can play the appropriate major blues scale.

Remember, the scale steps are from this scale. (For example, III in this key is a minor third up from the tonic.)

For A major blues	As Scale Steps
A7, D7, E7	I^7, IV^7, V^7
A, C, D, E	I, III, IV, V
A7, G	I^7, VII
A7, Bm, D7, E7	I^7, ii, IV^7, V^7

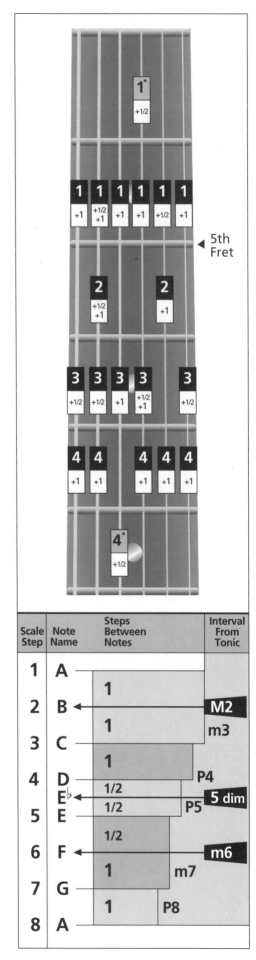

Scale Step	Note Name	Steps Between Notes	Interval From Tonic
1	A		
		1	
2	B		M2
		1	
3	C		m3
		1	
4	D		P4
		1/2	
5	E♭		5 dim
		1/2	P5
5	E		
		1/2	
6	F		m6
		1	m7
7	G		
		1	P8
8	A		

The minor blues scale takes a different departure from the normal blues scale than does the major blues scale. To form this scale, two notes are added to the normal blues scale— the major second and the minor sixth.

This scale is identical to the natural minor scale or Aeolian mode (see Minor Modes on page 16 and Aeolian Mode on page 18), the single exception being that the flatted fifth is present.

Record yourself playing an *A minor* chord (or have a friend play it). While the chord is playing, play these two examples:

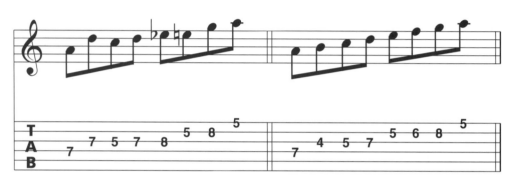

Notice that while the *A minor* chord imparts some of its "sad", minor quality to the lead, the second example also has a "jazzy" kind of feel to it, caused by the addition of the major second and minor sixth notes.

Here is tablature for the *A minor blues* scale shown in the charts at the left:

Notice that there is one note (B) that is shown on two strings in the tablature. This note may be played either place. This is also indicated on the chart (and will be in other charts) by shading that note grey instead of black in both locations, and placing an asterisk after the fingering number.

Standard guitar technique emphasizes choosing fingerings that pull *into* a position, rather than *away from* it. Thus, the most common use of the availability of two fingering choices for the B note we have been discussing is to play it on the third string when ascending (playing the first finger twice, first out of position and then in position) and on the fourth string descending. For example:

Here is a table showing which minor blues scale you are playing at all the positions available on a 22-fret guitar. (Positions 20 and above would be incomplete and are therefore omitted.)

POSITION	SCALE
open	E minor blues scale
1	F minor blues scale
2	F#/G♭ minor blues scale
3	G minor blues scale
4	G#/A♭ minor blues scale
5	A minor blues scale
6	A#/B♭ minor blues scale
7	B minor blues scale
8	C minor blues scale
9	C#/D♭ minor blues scale
10	D minor blues scale
11	D#/E♭ minor blues scale
12	E minor blues scale
13	F minor blues scale
14	F#/G♭ minor blues scale
15	G minor blues scale
16	G#/A♭ minor blues scale
17	A minor blues scale
18	A#/B♭ minor blues scale
19	B minor blues scale

Below is a table showing some typical chord progressions for minor blues keys, both for the key of *A minor blues* and as scale steps. When you encounter these progressions, you can play the appropriate minor blues scale.

Remember, the scale steps are from this scale. (For example, III in this key is a minor third up from the tonic.)

For A minor blues	As Scale Steps
Am7, Dm7, Em7	i[7], iv[7], v[7]
Am, C, Dm, Em	i, III, iv, v
Am, G	i, VII

Minor Modes

*T*he modes are a series of related scales — they all contain the same notes (and therefore generate the same chords). What differs from one mode to the next is which note is considered the tonic.

While this may seem like a small difference, in practice it is a huge one. The difference in "feel" between a Van Morrison song such as "Moondance" and a Lynyrd Skynyrd song such as "Sweet Home Alabama" is largely due to their being in different modes.

In the next several sections of this book, we are going to explore modes. In the interest of clarity, we will use as examples the seven modes that contain the same notes as a *C major* scale. They are:

- C Ionian (or C major)

- D Dorian

- E Phrygian

- F Lydian

- G Mixolydian

- A Aeolian (or natural minor)

- B Locrian

This is called the **C major family of modes**. (Modal families are usually named for the major scale from which they are derived.)

Notice that each of these modes has a double name — a letter that indicates the first note and a name that indicates the type of mode. This is true of all scales, including Blues scales and altered scales.

When you deal with scales and modes, you are dealing with two important concepts — **tonality** and **modality**.

Tonality is concerned with only one thing — which of the notes is the tonic? This is extremely important to know, because all scales and modes refer to and usually resolve to the tonic. Thus, an *A blues* scale, an *A pentatonic* scale, an *A major* scale, an *A Lydian* scale, and any other scale that has the note A for a tonic are **A tonalities**.

Modality deals with another question — in what way do the notes in the scale relate to the tonic? This can be looked at in terms of distances between the notes (in steps and half-steps) or in terms of interval from the tonic. Both of these are shown in the "Steps/Intervals" charts given for each scale in this book. It follows, then that *A Lydian, C Lydian, E Lydian*, and any other 7 note scale that contains exactly that same sequence of half and whole steps from the tonic will be **Lydian modalities**.

Putting a tonality and a modality together gives you a **key**. A key will **always** refer to both a tonality and a modality. Thus, *A major, B minor, C Lydian, F Mixolydian*, etc. are all examples of keys, and all refer to both a tonality and a modality. (When you talk about the key of A, which does not appear to refer to a modality, you are actually using the common shorthand for the key of *A major*.)

If modes seem a bit confusing at first, consider this analogy. Let's say that you took a rubber ball, and divided its surface into seven even sections, painted each section a different color and wrote one of the letters from A through G in each section, without skipping or repeating any letters. Then let's say you threw it in a pool of water. (Assume that this ball floats in such a way that exactly 1/7th of its surface is above the water, and that it always reveals only one of the seven painted sections at a time, in its entirety, although it may turn as it floats and reveal different sections at different times.)

Now, suppose you had a few different friends look at this ball floating in the pool at different points in time . The first friend might say, "Oh, yeah, it's a red ball and it's got an 'A' written on it." The second might say,"No, it's a blue ball and there's a 'G' on it. A third might say, "You're both nuts, it's a green ball and it says 'D'."

Of, course, it's actually all the same ball. What differs is each person's perspective.

You may think of the part of the ball that floats above the surface of the water as being equivalent to the tonic of a mode. All of the relationships between the seven painted sections stay the same relative to each other, but an observer's perspective differs.

Diatonic triads may be constructed on modes, just as they are on a major scale. In fact, as we go through the modes from the *C major* family, you will notice that we keep finding the same seven triads, but on different number scale steps.

Three of the modes (Ionian, Mixolydian and Lydian) have major tonic chords, and three of them (Aeolian, Dorian and Phrygian) have minor tonic chords. These modes are usually referred to as major modes and minor modes, respectively. The seventh mode (Locrian) has a diminished tonic chord, is quite dissonant, and rarely appears other that in jazz/rock fusion.

We will begin examining the modes with the minor modes, because they can be easily formed by filling in the pentatonic shell that we already know, and therefore keep all the bending options in the same familiar and comfortable places.

We will take them in order of most common usage, beginning with the Aeolian or natural minor scale.

In addition to the "Shape", and Steps/Intervals" charts, the tablature for the scale and the table of fretboard locations, we will include tablature for the diatonic triads for each mode as we go along.

Also, instead of a table of **typical** chord progressions, we will include a table of **defining** chord progressions. This is again an important distinction. **Typical** progressions are ones that you might encounter in a given key, and may leave you several scale choices for improvising. For example, if you encounter a I - IV progression (such as A - D), you have a number of scale choices (*A blues, A major, A major blues*, etc).

A **defining** progression, on the other hand, is one that can occur only in one scale and nowhere else. (You may still choose to deliberately play a different scale to create a dissonant effect.) For example, a *i - iv - v* progression (such as *Am - Dm - Em*) can occur in only in one scale (*A Aeolian* or *natural minor*). No other scale contains these chord relationships.

Learning the defining progressions for each mode will help you greatly in finding the tonality and modality of any piece of music, and therefore in deciding what scales to use in your improvisational approach.

Aeolian Mode

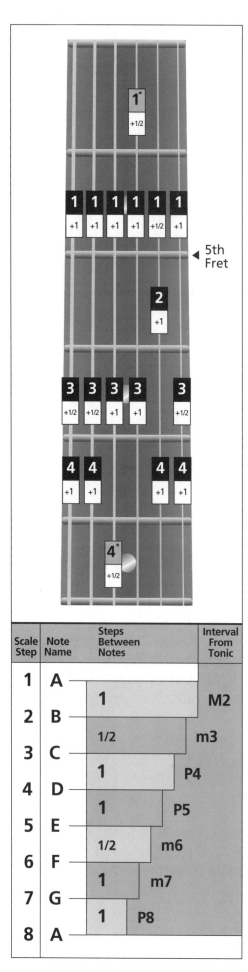

Scale Step	Note Name	Steps Between Notes	Interval From Tonic
1	A		
		1	M2
2	B		
		1/2	m3
3	C		
		1	P4
4	D		
		1	P5
5	E		
		1/2	m6
6	F		
		1	m7
7	G		
		1	P8
8	A		

*T*he most commonly used minor mode is the Aeolian mode (also known as the natural minor scale). Songs such as "All Along The Watchtower," and "Stairway To Heaven" are in Aeolian modes.

The Aeolian mode can be constructed by playing a major scale, but starting on the sixth scale step. In the *C major* family of modes, then, the *A Aeolian* scale may be derived by playing the seven notes of the *C major* scale, in sequence, but beginning on the sixth scale step, A, which becomes the new tonic.

Thus:

C major

1	2	3	4	5	6	7	8(1)	2	3	4	5	6
C	D	E	F	G	A	B	C	D	E	F	G	A
					1	2	3	4	5	6	7	8

A Aeolian

You can see then, that *1* in *A Aeolian* is the same note as *6* in *C major*, *2* in *A Aeolian* is the same note as *7* in *C major*, etc.

Here is tablature for the *A Aeolian* scale shown in the charts at the left:

Notice that this is the familiar minor pentatonic shell with the addition of the major second and the minor sixth. It is also identical to the minor blues scale, but without the flat-fifth note.

Remember that the B note in the second octave may be played on either the fourth string (at the ninth fret) or the third string (at the fourth fret).

Because this scale has the note A for its tonic, it gives rise to a different set of diatonic triad relationships, even though the chords all remain in the same step/interval relationships to each other that they are in the *C major* scale.

Here are the diatonic triads for the *A Aeolian* scale. Notice that just as the Aeolian scale contains the same notes as a *C major* scale, in the same sequence, but starting at a different place; these are the same triads as the *C major* diatonic triads, in the same sequence, but starting at a different place.

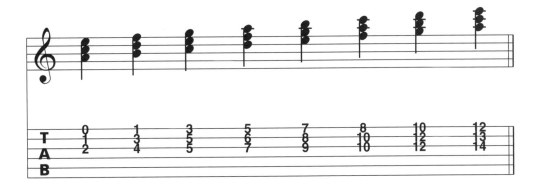

Here is a table showing which Aeolian scale you are playing at all the positions available on a 22-fret guitar. (Positions 20 and above would be incomplete and are therefore omitted.)

POSITION	SCALE
open	E Aeolian mode
1	F Aeolian mode
2	F#/Gb Aeolian mode
3	G Aeolian mode
4	G#/Ab Aeolian mode
5	A Aeolian mode
6	A#/Bb Aeolian mode
7	B Aeolian mode
8	C Aeolian mode
9	C#/Db Aeolian mode
10	D Aeolian mode
11	D#/Eb Aeolian mode
12	E Aeolian mode
13	F Aeolian mode
14	F#/Gb Aeolian mode
15	G Aeolian mode
16	G#/Ab Aeolian mode
17	A Aeolian mode
18	A#/Bb Aeolian mode
19	B Aeolian mode

Below is a table showing some defining chord progressions for Aeolian keys, both for the key of *A Aeolian* and as scale steps. When you encounter these progressions, you **must** be in an Aeolian key.

Remember, the scale steps are from this scale. (For example, III in this key is a minor third up from the tonic.)

For A Aeolian	As Scale Steps
Am, Dm, Em	i, iv, v
Am, C, Dm, Em	i, III, iv, v
Am, G, F	i, VII, VI

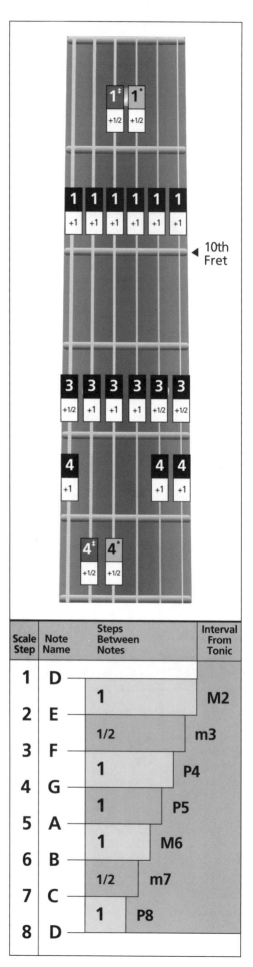

Scale Step	Note Name	Steps Between Notes	Interval From Tonic
1	D		
		1	M2
2	E		
		1/2	m3
3	F		
		1	P4
4	G		
		1	P5
5	A		
		1	M6
6	B		
		1/2	m7
7	C		
		1	P8
8	D		

*T*he second most commonly used minor mode is the Dorian mode. Songs such as "Moondance," and "Oye Como Va" are in Dorian modes. (In fact, much of Santana's music is in Dorian modes.)

The Dorian mode can be constructed by playing a major scale, but starting on the second scale step. In the *C major* family of modes, then, the *D Dorian* scale may be derived by playing the seven notes of the *C major* scale, in sequence, but beginning on the second scale step, D, which becomes the new tonic.

Thus:

C major

1	2	3	4	5	6	7	8(1)	2
C	D	E	F	G	A	B	C	D
	1	2	3	4	5	6	7	8

D Dorian

You can see then, that *1* in *D Dorian* is the same note as *2* in *C major*, *2* in *D Dorian* is the same note as *3* in *C major*, etc.

Here is tablature for the *D Dorian scale* shown in the charts at the left:

Notice that this is again the familiar minor pentatonic shell with the addition of the major second and the major sixth.

In addition to the the E note in the second octave that may be played on either the fourth string (at the fourteenth fret) or the third string (at the ninth fret), the B note in the first octave may be played on either the fifth string (at the fourteenth fret) or the fourth string (at the ninth fret)

Because this scale has the note D for its tonic, it gives rise to a different set of diatonic triad relationships, even though the chords all remain in the same step/interval relationships to each other that they are in the *C major* scale.

Here are the diatonic triads for the *D Dorian* scale. Notice that just as this Dorian scale contains the same notes as a *C major* scale, in the same sequence, but starting at a different place; these are the same triads as the *C major* diatonic triads, in the same sequence, but starting at a different place.

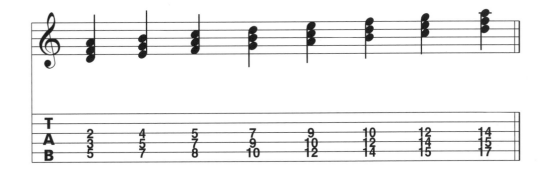

Here is a table showing which Dorian scale you are playing at all the positions available on a 22-fret guitar. (Positions 20 and above would be incomplete and are therefore omitted.)

POSITION	SCALE
open	E Dorian mode
1	F Dorian mode
2	F#/G♭ Dorian mode
3	G Dorian mode
4	G#/A♭ Dorian mode
5	A Dorian mode
6	A#/B♭ Dorian mode
7	B Dorian mode
8	C Dorian mode
9	C#/D♭ Dorian mode
10	D Dorian mode
11	D#/E♭ Dorian mode
12	E Dorian mode
13	F Dorian mode
14	F#/G♭ Dorian mode
15	G Dorian mode
16	G#/A♭ Dorian mode
17	A Dorian mode
18	A#/B♭ Dorian mode
19	B Dorian mode

Below is a table showing some defining chord progressions for Dorian keys, both for the key of *D Dorian* and as scale steps. When you encounter these progressions, you **must** be in a Dorian key.

Remember, the scale steps are from this scale. (For example, III in this key is a minor third up from the tonic.)

For D Dorian	As Scale Steps
Dm, Em	i, ii
Dm, G7	i, IV⁷
Dm, C, G7	i, VII, IV⁷

Phrygian Mode

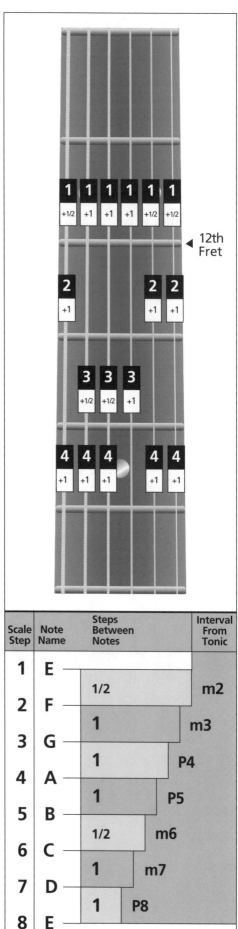

Scale Step	Note Name	Steps Between Notes		Interval From Tonic
1	E			
		1/2		m2
2	F			
		1		m3
3	G			
		1		P4
4	A			
		1		P5
5	B			
		1/2		m6
6	C			
		1		m7
7	D			
		1		P8
8	E			

*T*he third minor mode is the Phrygian mode. Songs such as "White Rabbit" and "House at Pooneil Corner" (both by the *Jefferson Airplane*) are in Phrygian modes.

The Phrygian mode can be constructed by playing a major scale, but starting on the third scale step. In the *C major* family of modes, then, the *E Phrygian* scale may be derived by playing the seven notes of the *C major* scale, in sequence, but beginning on the third scale step, E, which becomes the new tonic.

Thus:

C major

1	2	3	4	5	6	7	8(1)	2	3
C	D	E	F	G	A	B	C	D	E
		1	2	3	4	5	6	7	8

E Phrygian

You can see then, that *1* in *E Phrygian* is the same note as *3* in *C major*, *2* in *E Phrygian* is the same note as *4* in *C major*, etc.

Here is tablature for the *E Phrygian* scale shown in the charts at the left:

Notice that this is again the familiar minor pentatonic shell with the addition of the minor second and the minor sixth..

Unlike the Aeolian and Dorian shapes, this Phrygian shape contains no notes that fall out of position or may be played in more than one place.

Because this scale has the note E for its tonic, it gives rise to a different set of diatonic triad relationships, even though the chords all remain in the same step/interval relationships to each other that they are in the *C major* scale.

Here are the diatonic triads for the *E Phrygian* scale. Notice that just as the Phrygian scale contains the same notes as a *C major* scale, in the same sequence, but starting at a different place; these are the same triads as the *C major* diatonic triads, in the same sequence, but starting at a different place.

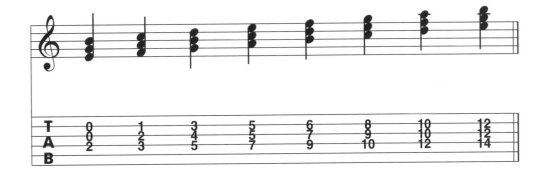

Here is a table showing which Phrygian scale you are playing at all the positions available on a 22-fret guitar. (Positions 20 and above would be incomplete and are therefore omitted.)

POSITION	SCALE
open	E Phrygian mode
1	F Phrygian mode
2	F#/G♭ Phrygian mode
3	G Phrygian mode
4	G#/A♭ Phrygian mode
5	A Phrygian mode
6	A#/B♭ Phrygian mode
7	B Phrygian mode
8	C Phrygian mode
9	C#/D♭ Phrygian mode
10	D Phrygian mode
11	D#/E♭ Phrygian mode
12	E Phrygian mode
13	F Phrygian mode
14	F#/G♭ Phrygian mode
15	G Phrygian mode
16	G#/A♭ Phrygian mode
17	A Phrygian mode
18	A#/B♭ Phrygian mode
19	B Phrygian mode

Below is a table showing some defining chord progressions for Phrygian keys, both for the key of *E Phrygian* and as scale steps. When you encounter these progressions, you **must** be in a Phrygian key.

Remember, the scale steps are from this scale. (For example, II in this key is a minor second up from the tonic.)

For E Phrygian	As Scale Steps
Em, F	i, II

Major Modes

*T*he three minor modes that we have just examined all share a common base — they each consist of a minor pentatonic shell with two additional notes added to complete the scale, thus preserving shapes and bend positions that are familiar and easy to use. The major modes differ in that they are not built from minor pentatonic shells.

It is helpful to remember that these modes are called major modes because the diatonic triad built on the tonic is a major chord. When you are trying to determine the correct mode for a piece of music, the first thing to consider (after finding the tonic note) is whether the tonic chord is major or minor.

The major modes all make use of out-of-position notes — each mode encompasses five (rather than four) frets. And they all make use of the "big stretch." Here is tablature for a big stretch beginning on the C note found on the sixth string at the eight fret.

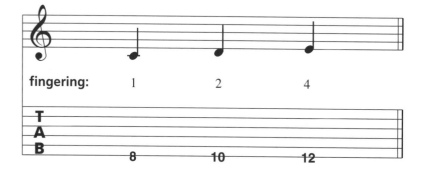

Notice the fingering — there is a stretch of one extra fret between your first finger (which is fretting the eighth fret) and your second finger (which is fretting the tenth fret). This is typical of the stretches found in all of the major modes that will be presented.

The best way to approach this stretch is to treat it as if the underlying position is one fret higher than the first note of the scale. In the example above, treat the scale as if it were in the **ninth** position (not the eighth position).

Here are a few things to keep in mind about positions and position playing:

- a position is group of four frets (one for each finger)

- it is named for the fret played by the index finger of the fret hand. (If your index finger is fretting the fifth fret, you are in fifth position, if it is fretting the seventh fret, you are in the seventh position, etc.)

- even though the position is named for the normal position of the first finger, the position of the thumb (which should be behind the second finger) actually determines which position is being played.

Look at the following example:

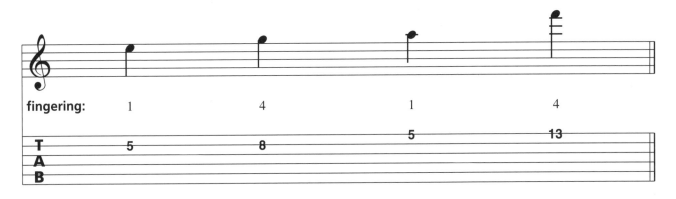

There are two ways to approach this example:

- Leave your thumb behind the ninth fret, and pivot the fret hand to place the little finger on the thirteenth fret. (You are staying in the eighth position and reaching out of position.) This is the best approach if the music you are playing continues in the eighth position after the out-of-position note.

- Move the thumb up the neck so that it is behind the eleventh fret as you place your little finger on the thirteenth fret. (You are shifting to the tenth position.) This is the best approach if the music you are playing continues in the tenth position after the F note at thirteenth fret.

Again, when playing big stretches, treat them as if the position is one fret higher than the first note played by the index finger would lead you to believe. If the first note of a big stretch is at the eighth fret, play in the ninth position and reach back for the first note. Do not shift the thumb or move the whole hand to play a big stretch — leave the thumb and hand stationary and reach back with the index finger for the out-of-position notes.

Here is an exercise to help you with big stretches:

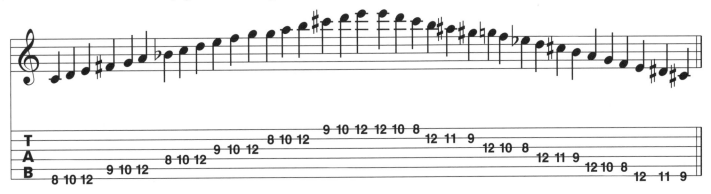

Use fingers 1, 2 and 4 ascending. Use fingers 1, 2 and 4 for the big stretches (strings 1, 3 and 5) and fingers 1, 3 and 4 for the in-position notes (strings 2, 4 and 6) descending.

Ionian Mode

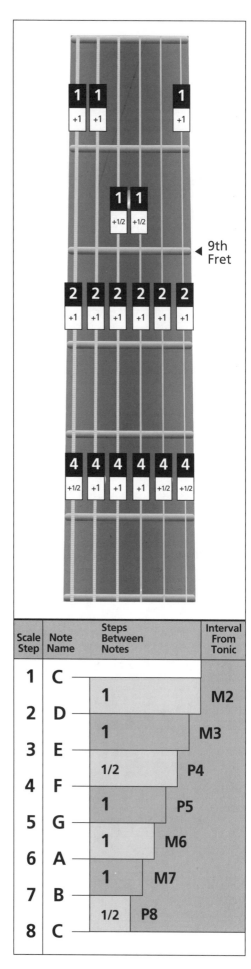

9th Fret

Scale Step	Note Name	Steps Between Notes	Interval From Tonic
1	C		
2	D	1	M2
3	E	1	M3
4	F	1/2	P4
5	G	1	P5
6	A	1	M6
7	B	1	M7
8	C	1/2	P8

*T*he most commonly used major mode is the Ionian mode (also known as the major scale). Songs such as "Ramblin' Man" and "Alison" are in Ionian modes (a lot of country music is also in Ionian modes)

The Ionian mode is identical to a major scale In the *C major* family of modes, then, the *C Ionian* scale may be derived by playing the seven notes of the *C major* scale, in sequence

Thus:

			C major				
1	*2*	*3*	*4*	*5*	*6*	*7*	*8(1)*
C	**D**	**E**	**F**	**G**	**A**	**B**	**C**
1	2	3	4	5	6	7	8
			C Ionian				

You can see then, that *1* in *C Ionian* is the same note as *1* in *C major*, *2* in *C Ionian* is the same note as *2* in *C major*, etc.

Here is tablature for the *C Ionian* scale shown in the charts at the left:

Notice the big stretches on strings six, five and one. When playing these, try to keep your hand in the ninth position (with the thumb behind the tenth fret) and reach back to the eighth fret for the out-of-position notes.

Because this scale has the note C for its tonic, it gives rise to the same set of diatonic triad relationships as the *C major* scale.

Here are the diatonic triads for the *C Ionian* scale. Notice that these are the same triads as the *C major* diatonic triads, in the same sequence, starting at the same place.

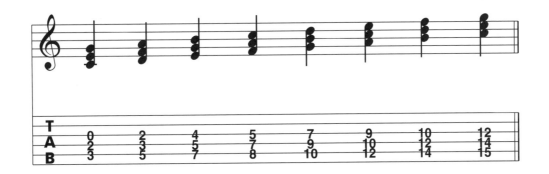

Here is a table showing which Ionian scale you are playing at all the positions available on a 22-fret guitar. (Positions 20 and above would be incomplete and are therefore omitted.)

POSITION	SCALE
open	E Ionian mode
1	F Ionian mode
2	F#/G♭ Ionian mode
3	G Ionian mode
4	G#/A♭ Ionian mode
5	A Ionian mode
6	A#/B♭ Ionian mode
7	B Ionian mode
8	C Ionian mode
9	C#/D♭ Ionian mode
10	D Ionian mode
11	D#/E♭ Ionian mode
12	E Ionian mode
13	F Ionian mode
14	F#/G♭ Ionian mode
15	G Ionian mode
16	G#/A♭ Ionian mode
17	A Ionian mode
18	A#/B♭ Ionian mode
19	B Ionian mode

Below is a table showing some defining chord progressions for Ionian (major) keys, both for the key of *C Ionian* (*C major*) and as scale steps. When you encounter these progressions, you **must** be in an Ionian (major) key.

Remember, the scale steps are from this scale. (For example, iii in this key is a major third up from the tonic.)

For C Ionian	As Scale Steps
C, F, G7	I, IV, V[7]
Dm, G7, C	ii, V[7], i
C, Am, Dm, G7	I, vi, ii, V[7]

Mixolydian Mode

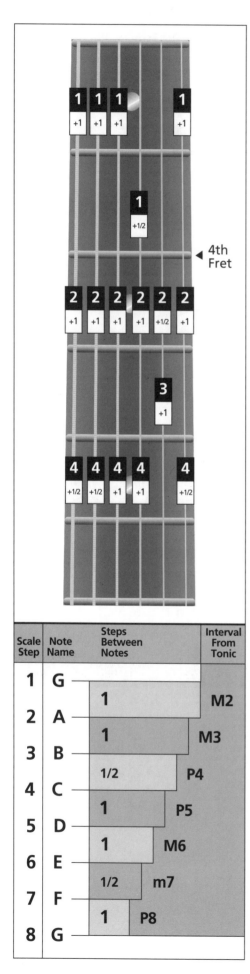

Scale Step	Note Name	Steps Between Notes		Interval From Tonic
1	G			
2	A	1		M2
3	B	1		M3
4	C	1/2		P4
5	D	1		P5
6	E	1		M6
7	F	1/2		m7
8	G	1		P8

*T*he second most commonly used major mode is the Mixolydian mode. Songs such as "Sweet Home Alabama" and "Dark Star" are in Mixolydian modes. (Much of the *Grateful Dead*'s music, and a lot of Irish music are in Mixolydian modes.)

The Mixolydian mode can be constructed by playing a major scale, but starting on the fifth scale step. In the *C major* family of modes, then, the *G Mixolydian* scale may be derived by playing the seven notes of the *C major* scale, in sequence, but beginning on the fifth scale step, G, which becomes the new tonic.

Thus:

C major

1	2	3	4	5	6	7	8(1)	2	3	4	5
C	D	E	F	G	A	B	C	D	E	F	G
				1	2	3	4	5	6	7	8

G Mixolydian

You can see then, that *1* in *G Mixolydian* is the same note as *5* in *C major*, *2* in *G Mixolydian* is the same note as *6* in *C major*, etc.

Here is tablature for the *G Mixolydian* scale shown in the charts at the left:

Notice the big stretches on strings six, five, four and one. When playing these, try to keep your hand in the fourth position (with the thumb behind the fifth fret) and reach back to the third fret for the out-of-position notes.

Because this scale has the note G for its tonic, it gives rise to a different set of diatonic triad relationships, even though the chords all remain in the same step/interval relationships to each other that they are in the *C major* scale.

Here are the diatonic triads for the *G Mixolydian* scale. Notice that just as the Mixolydian scale contains the same notes as a *C major* scale, in the same sequence, but starting at a different place; these are the same triads as the *C major* diatonic triads, in the same sequence, but starting at a different place.

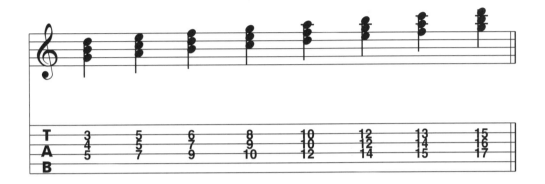

Here is a table showing which Mixolydian scale you are playing at all the positions available on a 22-fret guitar. (Positions 20 and above would be

Below is a table showing some defining chord progressions for Mixolydian keys, both for the key of *G Mixolydian* and as scale steps. When you encounter these progressions, you **must** be in a Mixolydian key.

Remember, the scale steps are from this scale. (For example, iii in this key is a major third up from the tonic.)

POSITION	SCALE
open	E Mixolydian mode
1	F Mixolydian mode
2	F♯/G♭ Mixolydian mode
3	G Mixolydian mode
4	G♯/A♭ Mixolydian mode
5	A Mixolydian mode
6	A♯/B♭ Mixolydian mode
7	B Mixolydian mode
8	C Mixolydian mode
9	C♯/D♭ Mixolydian mode
10	D Mixolydian mode
11	D♯/E♭ Mixolydian mode
12	E Mixolydian mode
13	F Mixolydian mode
14	F♯/G♭ Mixolydian mode
15	G Mixolydian mode
16	G♯/A♭ Mixolydian mode
17	A Mixolydian mode
18	A♯/B♭ Mixolydian mode
19	B Mixolydian mode

For G Mixolydian	As Scale Steps
G, F, C	I, VII, IV
G, F	I, VII

Lydian Mode

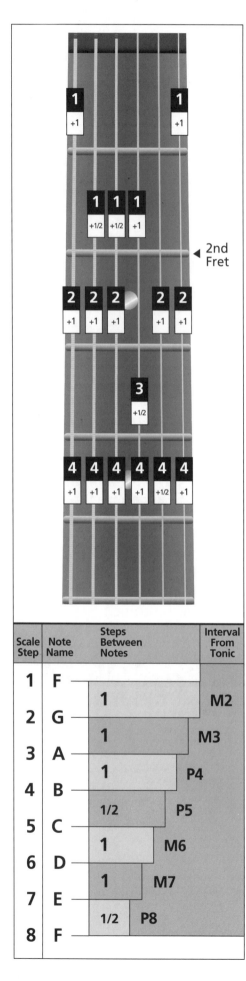

Scale Step	Note Name	Steps Between Notes	Interval From Tonic
1	F		
2	G	1	M2
3	A	1	M3
4	B	1	P4
5	C	1/2	P5
6	D	1	M6
7	E	1	M7
8	F	1/2	P8

*T*he third major mode is the Lydian mode. Songs such as "Devotion" and "Everybody Wants To Rule The World" are in Lydian modes. (Lydian modes are also frequently used in jazz and fusion music.)

The Lydian mode can be constructed by playing a major scale, but starting on the fourth scale step. In the *C major* family of modes, then, the *F Lydian* scale may be derived by playing the seven notes of the *C major* scale, in sequence, but beginning on the fourth scale step, F, which becomes the new tonic.

Thus:

C major

1	2	3	4	5	6	7	8(1)	2	3	4
C	D	E	F	G	A	B	C	D	E	F
			1	2	3	4	5	6	7	8

F Lydian

You can see then, that *1* in *F Lydian* is the same note as *4* in *C major*, *2* in *F Lydian* is the same note as *5* in *C major*, etc.

Here is tablature for the *F Lydian* scale shown in the charts at the left:

Notice the big stretches on strings six and one. When playing these, try to keep your hand in the second position (with the thumb behind the third fret) and reach back to the first fret for the out-of-position notes.

Because this scale has the note F for its tonic, it gives rise to a different set of diatonic triad relationships, even though the chords all remain in the same step/interval relationships to each other that they are in the *C major* scale.

Here are the diatonic triads for the *F Lydian* scale. Notice that just as the Lydian scale contains the same notes as a *C major* scale, in the same sequence, but starting at a different place; these are the same triads as the *C major* diatonic triads, in the same sequence, but starting at a different place.

Here is a table showing which Lydian scale you are playing at all the positions available on a 22-fret guitar. (Positions 20 and above would be incomplete and are therefore omitted.)

POSITION	SCALE
open	E Lydian mode
1	F Lydian mode
2	F#/G♭ Lydian mode
3	G Lydian mode
4	G#/A♭ Lydian mode
5	A Lydian mode
6	A#/B♭ Lydian mode
7	B Lydian mode
8	C Lydian mode
9	C#/D♭ Lydian mode
10	D Lydian mode
11	D#/E♭ Lydian mode
12	E Lydian mode
13	F Lydian mode
14	F#/G♭ Lydian mode
15	G Lydian mode
16	G#/A♭ Lydian mode
17	A Lydian mode
18	A#/B♭ Lydian mode
19	B Lydian mode

Below is a table showing some defining chord progressions for Lydian keys, both for the key of *F Lydian* and as scale steps. When you encounter these progressions, you **must** be in a Lydian key.

Remember, the scale steps are from this scale. (For example, iii in this key is a minor third up from the tonic.)

For F Lydian	As Scale Steps
F, G	I, II

Locrian Mode

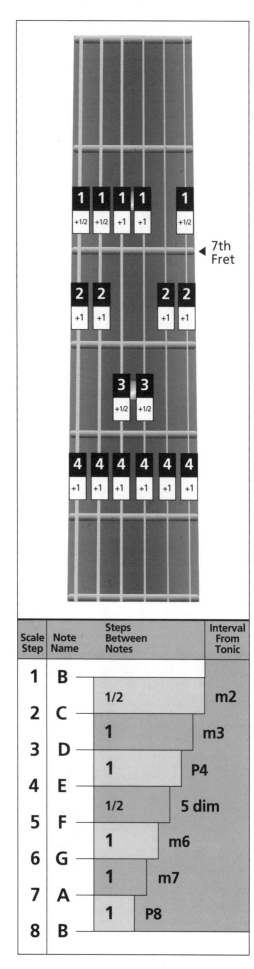

Scale Step	Note Name	Steps Between Notes	Interval From Tonic
1	B		
		1/2	m2
2	C		
		1	m3
3	D		
		1	P4
4	E		
		1/2	5 dim
5	F		
		1	m6
6	G		
		1	m7
7	A		
		1	P8
8	B		

The last mode is the Locrian mode, which is not considered either major or minor, due to the diminished triad that falls on the tonic. This mode seldom appears outside of fusion music.

The Locrian mode can be constructed by playing a major scale, but starting on the seventh scale step. In the *C major* family of modes, then, the *B Locrian* scale may be derived by playing the seven notes of the *C major* scale, in sequence, but beginning on the seventh scale step, B, which becomes the new tonic.

Thus:

							C major						
1	*2*	*3*	*4*	*5*	*6*	*7*	*8(1)*	*2*	*3*	*4*	*5*	*6*	*7*
C	D	E	F	G	A	B	C	D	E	F	G	A	B
							1	2	3	4	5	6	7	8

B Locrian

You can see then, that *1* in *B Locrian* is the same note as *7* in *C major*, *2* in *B Locrian* is the same note as *1* in *C major*, etc.

Here is tablature for the *B Locrian* scale shown in the charts at the left:

While this is similar to a filled pentatonic shell in shape, it is missing the first finger note on the second string. It does not, however, contain any big stretches.

Because this scale has the note B for its tonic, it gives rise to a different set of diatonic triad relationships, even though the chords all remain in the same step/interval relationships to each other that they are in the *C major* scale.

Here are the diatonic triads for the *B Locrian* scale. Notice that just as the Locrian scale contains the same notes as a *C major* scale, in the same sequence, but starting at a different place; these are the same triads as the *C major* diatonic triads, in the same sequence, but starting at a different place.

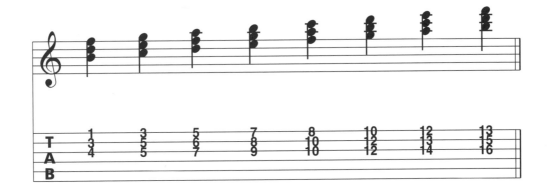

Here is a table showing which Locrian scale you are playing at all the positions available on a 22-fret guitar. (Positions 20 and above would be incomplete and are therefore omitted.)

POSITION	SCALE
open	E Locrian mode
1	F Locrian mode
2	F#/G♭ Locrian mode
3	G Locrian mode
4	G#/A♭ Locrian mode
5	A Locrian mode
6	A#/B♭ Locrian mode
7	B Locrian mode
8	C Locrian mode
9	C#/D♭ Locrian mode
10	D Locrian mode
11	D#/E♭ Locrian mode
12	E Locrian mode
13	F Locrian mode
14	F#/G♭ Locrian mode
15	G Locrian mode
16	G#/A♭ Locrian mode
17	A Locrian mode
18	A#/B♭ Locrian mode
19	B Locrian mode

Here is a table showing some defining chord progressions for Locrian keys, both for the key of *B Locrian* and as scale steps. When you encounter these progressions, you **must** be in a Locrian key.

Remember, the scale steps are from this scale. (For example, II in this key is a minor second up from the tonic.)

For B Locrian	As Scale Steps
B°	i°

Knowing a lot of scales and shapes is useful only if you know how to use them. The rest of this book will deal with different ways of using the scales you know. We will begin by dealing with the relationship between a major scale and its relative minor.

Record yourself playing a C major chord (or have another guitarist play it.) While the C chord is playing, play this:

You are playing a *C major* scale against a *C major* chord. It is easy to hear the characteristic major sound in this example.

Now record yourself playing an *A minor* chord (or have another guitarist play it) and play the same example while the *A minor* chord is playing.

What happened ??? You no longer hear that major sound!!! None of the notes sound wrong, but the whole "feel" of the music has changed.

What has happened is this: by changing the chord, you have changed the key. (Remember that a key refers to both a tonality and a modality.) Chords **always** rule melodies. That is simply how human hearing works. There is nothing that you can do melodically when that *A minor* chord is playing to make the overall effect of the music be major (or anything other than minor).

Why does the *C major* scale sound good (although different) while the *A minor* chord is playing?? Because *A minor* is the **relative minor** to *C major*, and, as such, contains the same notes as *C major*.

A minor (actually, *A natural minor*) is identical to the *A Aeolian* mode that we learned earlier. It contains the same notes as the *C major* scale, but starts from the sixth step:

					C major							
1	2	3	4	5	6	7	8(1)	2	3	4	5	6
C	D	E	F	G	A	B	C	D	E	F	G	A
					1	2	3	4	5	6	7	8
					A minor							

Every major scale has a relative minor scale, and the relationship between the two is always the same. This is very important information, because, as you will see shortly, it is this relationship that will be the most useful to you as a guitarist.

In the same way that you can think of *A minor* as the relative minor of *C major*, you may think of *C major* as the *relative major* of *A minor*. It contains the same notes as the *A minor* scale, but begins on the third step:

						A minor			
1	*2*	*3*	*4*	*5*	*6*	*7*	*8(1)*	*2*	*3*
A	**B**	**C**	**D**	**E**	**F**	**G**	**A**	**B**	**C**
		1	2	3	4	5	6	7	8
						C major			

The important thing to see here, is that whether you call this group of notes *A minor* or *C major*, it is still the same 7 notes. And the thing that will decide for you which to call it is the chords.

C major (which is identical to the *C Ionian* mode) has certain defining chord relationships. It is the only key that contains a *major I* chord, a *major IV* chord **and** a *major V* chord. It is the only key that can have a *V7* chord. It is the only key that contains a *minor ii* chord, a dominant-type seventh *V* chord(V7) **and** a *major I* chord.

A minor (which is identical to the *A Aeolian* mode) also has certain defining chord relationships. It is the only key that contains a *minor i* chord, a *minor iv* chord **and** a *minor v* chord. It is the only key that can have a *VII7* chord. It is the only key that contains a *major VI* chord, a *major VII* chord **and** a *minor i* chord.

If you encounter any of these chord progressions in a piece of music, they immediately tell you the key. For example "Stairway to Heaven" (from the guitar solo to the end) consists mostly of *F major*, *G major* and *A minor* chords, and *A minor* is the tonic.

> F major = VI
> G major = VII
> A minor = i

Thus it is in the key of *A minor*.

The verses of "Ramblin' Man" consist of *G major*, *C major*, *D major* and *E minor* chords, with *G* as the tonic. (The tonic is usually the ending chord in a piece of music.)

> G major = I
> C major = IV
> D major = V
> E minor = vi

Thus, it is in the key of *G major*.

Here is a table of the twelve major keys and their relative minors. Remember that this is a two-way relationship — you can also look at this as a table of minor keys and their relative majors.

RELATIVE MAJORS / MINORS	
C major	A minor
C$\sharp$/D$\flat$ major	A$\sharp$/B$\flat$ minor
D major	B minor
D$\sharp$/E$\flat$ major	B$\sharp$/C minor
E major	C$\sharp$ minor
F major	D minor
F$\sharp$/G$\flat$ major	D$\sharp$/E$\flat$ minor
G major	E minor
G$\sharp$/A$\flat$ major	E$\sharp$/F minor
A major	F$\sharp$ minor
A$\sharp$/B$\flat$ major	F$^{\times}$/G minor
B major	G$\sharp$ minor

The most important way that the concept of relative majors/minors is useful to you as a guitarist is this: it gives you a choice about where to play lead.

For example, if you are playing with a piece of music in the key of *C major*, you can use either the *C major* (*Ionian*) scale (which starts at the eight fret) or the *A minor* (*Aeolian*) scale (which starts at the fifth fret as places to work. Or you can switch from one to the other.

For example, here is a chord progression with a lead that is played out of the C major scale::

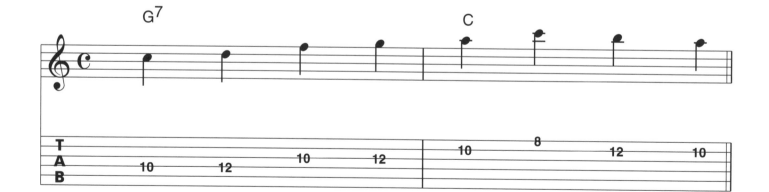

Here is the same chord progression, but now the lead is played out of the *A minor* position:

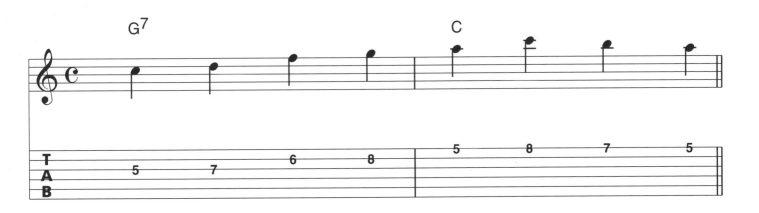

Finally, here is the same progression with a lead that switches from the *C major* position to the *A minor* position.

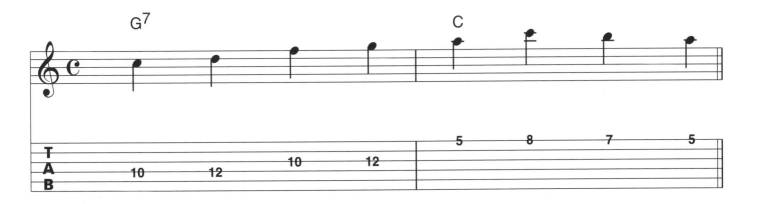

Notice that whether you play out of the *C major* position or the *A minor* position, the chords still determine the key — *C major*. The chords always determine the key. Then, you choose where to play — the position suggested by the key (in this case, *C major*), or the relative minor (in this case, *A minor*).

Next, notice that the *A minor* position is three frets below the *C major* position. This is a relationship that is always true. For any major position, the relative minor position is three frets lower.

Finally, remember that the minor scale is a filled pentatonic, which means that you can play the pentatonic instead of the full minor scale. This will give you a slightly different "feel" to use in your soloing, than either the full major scale or the full relative minor scale.

Relative Modes

*J*ust as a relative minor scale contains the same notes as its relative major, and can therefore be used in its place as a position for soloing, all of a major scale's relative modes contain the same notes as the relative major, and can be used as additional soloing positions.

Here is a chord progression with a lead from the *C major (Ionian)* position:

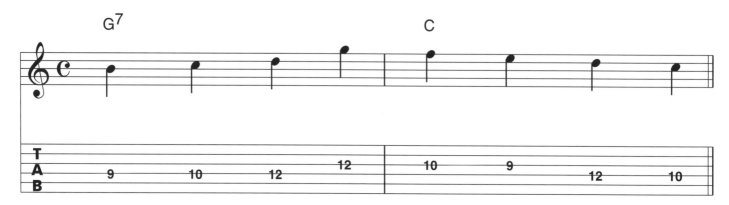

Here is the same progression with a lead from the *A minor (Aeolian)* position:

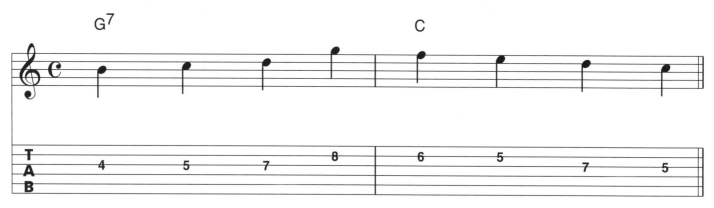

Here it is once again with a lead from the *E Phrygian* position:

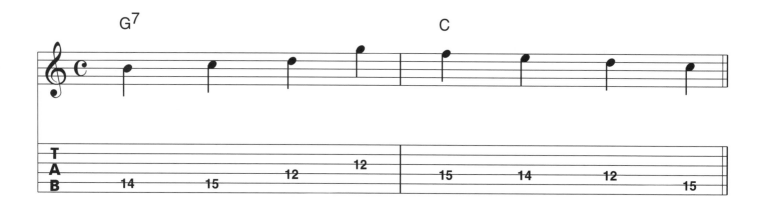

And again, with a lead from the *G Mixolydian* position:

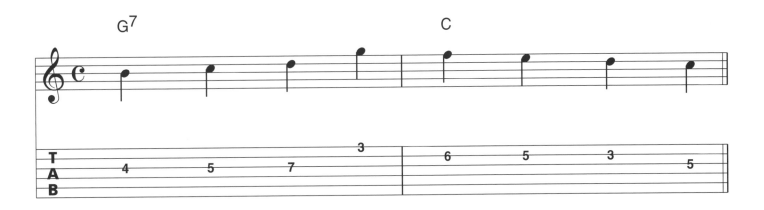

Any relative mode can be played in place of its relative major scale. In fact, any relative mode can be played in place of any other relative mode. This is true because of two things:

- They all contain the same notes. (The definition of relative modes is that they contain the same notes as each other, but each considers a different note to be the tonic, and therefore generates a different, characteristic set of chords.)

- The chords determine the key. (As we saw in the section on relative majors/minors, if the chords say C major, there is nothing that the melody or solo can do to make it be otherwise.)

Here is a table showing all of the relative modes for each of the twelve major key families. (For convenience, we name a family of modes for the major {Ionian} mode within that family.):

Major	Dorian	Phrygian	Lydian	Mixolydian	Aeolian	Locrian
C	D	E	F	G	A	B
C#/Db	D#/Eb	E#/F	F#/Gb	G#/Ab	A#/Bb	B#/C
D	E	F#	G	A	B	B
D#/Eb	E#/F	F*/G	G#/ab	A#/Bb	B#/C	C*/D
E	F#	G#	A	B	C#	D#
F	G	A	Bb	C	D	E
F#/Gb	G#/Ab	A#/Bb	B/Cb	C#/Db	D#/Eb	E*/f
G	A	B	C	D	E	F#
G#/Ab	A#/Bb	B#/C	C#/Db	D#/Eb	E#/F	F*/G
A	B	C#	D	E	F#	G#
A#/Bb	B#/C	C*/D	D#/Eb	E#/F	F*/G	G*/A
B	C#	D#	E	F#	G#	A#

Putting this concept to work, (using the *C major* family of modes once again, for convenience) here is a six-note lead played out of each of the modes with appropriate chords for that mode.

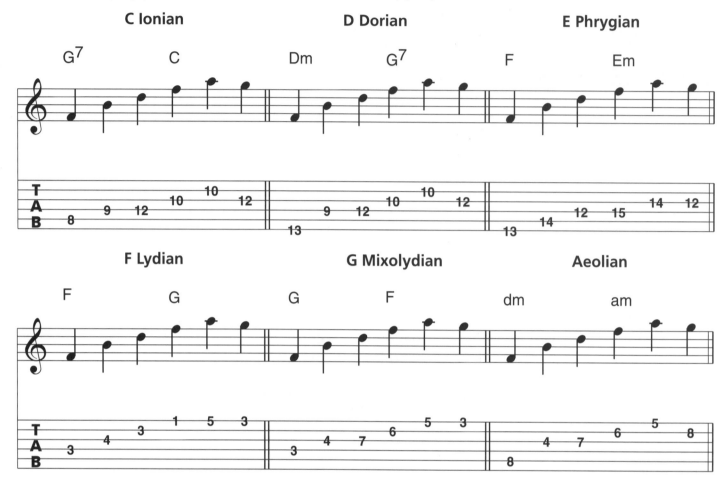

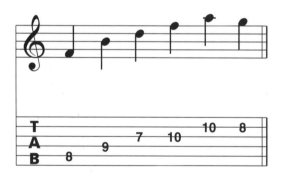

Since each of these examples contains the same notes, it is clear that any of the leads can be played with any of the chord sequences. This means that any time you are playing a piece of music (or a section of one) that is in one of the modes, you have seven scale patterns to choose from when making your note selections.

As a rock guitarist, you will find some of the choices more useful than others. For one thing, three of the modes (the three minor modes) are basically filled pentatonic shells, and therefore will be familiar to you, and will have bends that are easy and comfortable. Here, for example, is a bent note played out of each of the seven patterns:

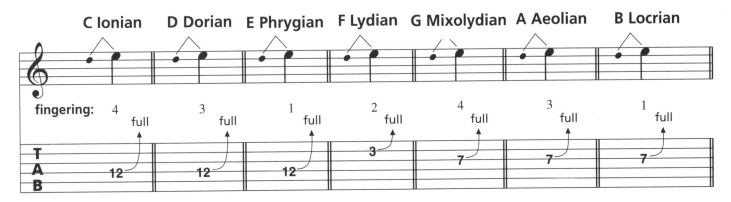

Notice that it is easier to play this bend in the Aeolian, Dorian and Phrygian patterns than in the others. This will also be true of most of the familiar pentatonic scale bends that you know.

Since filled pentatonics are your first choices for lead patterns, another modal relationship must be examined. Just as each major scale has its relative minor (and vice verse), each major mode has its relative minor mode. Here is a table showing each of these relationships:

RELATIVE MAJOR / MINOR MODES	
Ionian	Aeolian
Lydian	Dorian
Mixolydian	Phrygian

Notice that each relative minor mode pattern is (as in the relative major/minor relationship) three frets below its relative major mode pattern. This makes them, again, easy to find and familiar.

Here, finally, is a table showing the relative minor modes and their positions on the guitar for each of the twelve modal families.

Major	Aeolian	Fret(s)	Dorian	Fret(s)	APhrygian	Fret(s)
C	A	5,17	D	10	E	0,12
C#/D♭	A#/B♭	6,18	D#/E♭	11	E#/F	1,13
D	B	7	E	open, 12	F#	2,14
D#/E♭	B#/C	8	E#/F	1,13	F×/G	3,15
E	C#	9	F#	2,14	G#	4,16
F	D	10	G	3,15	A	5,17
F#/G♭	D#/E♭	11	G#/A♭	4,16	A#/B♭	6,18
G	E	open,12	A	5,17	B	7
G#/A♭	E#/F	1,13	A#/B♭	6,18	B#/C♭	8
A	F#/G♭	2,14	B	7	C#	9
A#/B♭	F×/G	3,15	B#/C	8	C×/D	10
B	G#	4,16	C#	9	D#	11

Parallel Modes

Relative modes, as we have just seen are very useful tools for playing music that is in any one key. Frequently, however, you will encounter music that changes keys. The verse, for example, might be in one key and the chorus in another, and the bridge in a third. Jazz compositions may change keys every few bars!!! Understanding parallel modes will help you find good ways to approach these key changes.

We already know that each modal family contains seven modes, all of which contain the same notes. Another way to look at modes is this: Each type of mode (Ionian, Dorian, Phrygian, Lydian, Mixolydian, Aeolian and Locrian) can be built upon any given note. Thus, while we call *C Ionian*, *D Dorian* and *E Phrygian*, etc. relative modes (because they contain the same notes) we call *C Ionian*, *C Dorian* and *C Phrygian*, etc. parallel modes (because they share the same tonic).

Parallel modes, while the share the same tonic, will never contain exactly the same notes as each other — there will always be at least one note that is different. They can, however be quite similar. For example, here is an *a Dorian* scale, an *A Phrygian* scale, an *A Aeolian* scale and, for reasons that you will see, an *A minor pentatonic* scale:

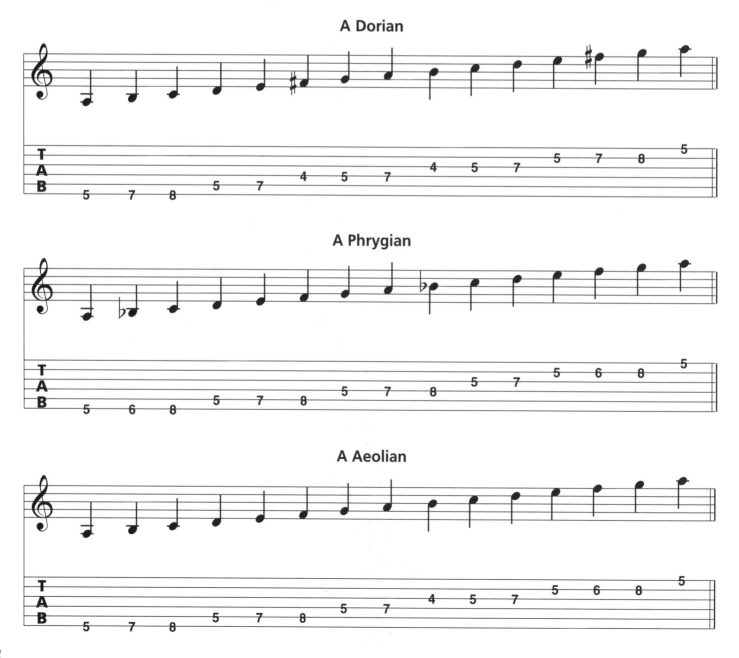

A minor pentatonic

Notice the following:

- The Dorian is the same as the Aeolian, except that the 6th step of the Dorian is a half-step higher than the 6th step in the Aeolian.

- The Phrygian is the same as the Aeolian, except that the 2nd step of the Phrygian is a half-step lower than the 2nd step in the Aeolian.

- The Dorian is the same as the Phrygian, except that the 2nd step of the Dorian is a half-step higher than the 2nd step in the Aeolian, and the 6th step of the Dorian is a half-step higher than the 6th step in the Phrygian.

- All of the notes in an *A minor pentatonic* scale can also be found in all three of these minor modes that begin on the note A.

Remember, that you can think of each of the minor modes as a pentatonic shell with two notes added. By changing which two notes you add, you can generate each of the three minor modes in any one position. Thus:

- Adding a major 2nd and a minor 6th to a minor pentatonic scale produces an Aeolian scale.

- Adding a major 2nd and a major 6th to a minor pentatonic scale produces a Dorian scale.

- Adding a minor 2nd and a minor 6th to a minor pentatonic scale produces a Phrygian scale.

Just as any three parallel minor modes differ from each other by only one or two notes, any three parallel major modes also differ from each other by only one or two notes.

Thus, clearly, if you know and understand parallel modes, you have a good set of tools for dealing effectively with key changes.

Parallel Modes (cont.)

Let's look at some parallel modes at work. Here is an *A Aeolian* chord progression and lead:

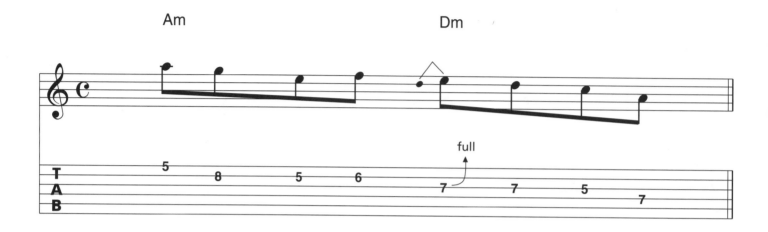

Here is the same thing, but in *D Aeolian*:

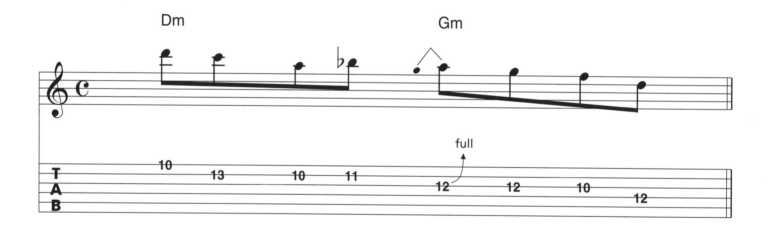

If you combine the two, you get this:

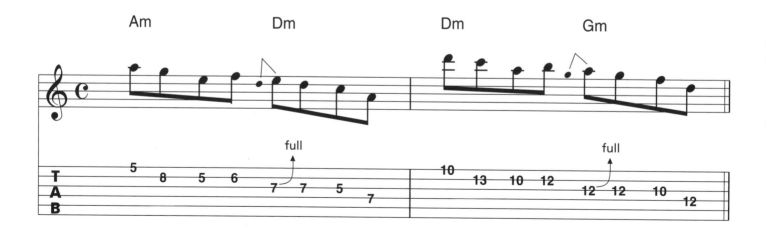

44

It is easy to hear the change from one mode to another in the preceding example — the lead guitar suddenly jumps to a new spot, rather than continuing in a smooth line.

If you examine the relative modes for each of the two sections, you will find the following:

A Aeolian	D Aeolian
A Aeolian	D Aeolian
B Locrian	E Locrian
C major	F lajor
D Dorian	G Dorian
E Phrygian	A Phrygian
F Lydian	B♭ Lydian
G Mixolydian	C Mixolydian

or, if you shift the table so that you start with identical tonics:

A Aeolian	D Aeolian
A Aeolian	A Phrygian
B Locrian	B♭ Lydian
C major	C Mixolydian
D Dorian	D Aeolian
E Phrygian	E Locrian
F Lydian	F major
G Mixolydian	G Dorian

Notice that other than the B note in the *a Aeolian* family differing from the Bb note in the *d Aeolian* family, all the other tonics are the same. If you stick exclusively to minor modes, for ease, you will see that you can play at either fifth fret (using the *a Aeolian / a Phrygian* combination) or at the 10th fret (using the *d Dorian / d Aeolian* combination) to play a lead that stays in one position as the key changes. This allows you to build smooth continuous lead lines. For example:

A Aeolian / A Phrygian

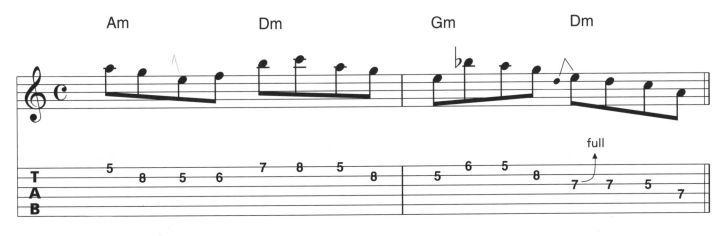

D Dorian / D Aeolian

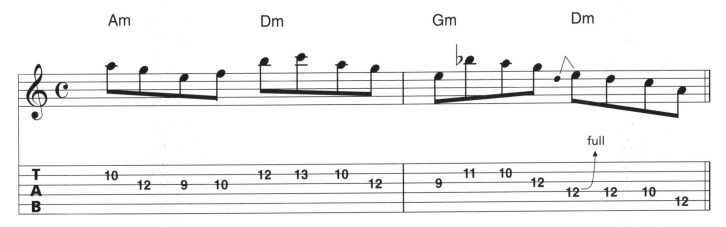

Horizontal Scales

All of the scales we have looked at in this book (and probably all of the ones that you have played) are what might be called **vertical** scales — they move up and down in pitch, but stay in one position on the guitar. (I call them vertical because the fret hand motion relative to the ground is up and down when you stay in one position.)

Knowing and playing all of these vertical scales, while giving you a variety of patterns and positions, is still not very helpful in creating smooth lines that use the entire fretboard. For that, we need to look at horizontal scales — scales that move up and down the neck on one string.

Here, for example is a portion of the *E Phrygian* scale that you already know:

Here is an *E Phrygian scale* played entirely on the first string (the fingering is important - two fingering choices are given for reasons that will become clear):

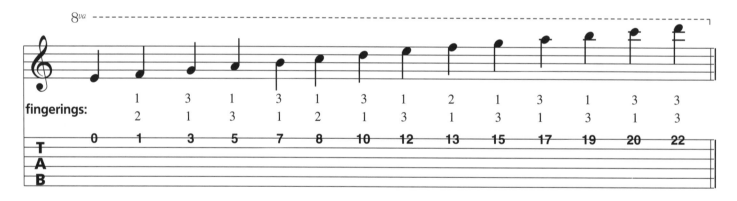

Once more, this time on second string:

46

Clearly all of the examples on the preceding page are the same mode, fingered in different ways. The horizontal modes, however, have one very important advantage — they move to and through all of the relative modes. Using *E Phrygian* as an example, here are all of the relative modes and the frets at which they occur:

Mode:	E Phrygian	F Lydian	G Mixolydian	A Aeolian	B Locrian	C Ionian	D Dorian
Fret:	open, 12	1,13	3,15	5, 17	7, 19	8	10

If you play the horizontal *E Phrygian* scale on the first string using only the 1st finger of the fret-hand, you are shifting from one modal patterns to the next. You could also (using the other fingering given) think of yourself as playing 2 notes in the open e Phrygian pattern, 2 notes in the 3rd fret *G Mixolydian* pattern, 2 notes in the 7th fret *B Locrian* position, etc. The possibilities are numerous.

However, as a rock guitarist, the most important ways to approach the horizontal scales is by using them to connect minor pentatonics. Using our *E Phrygian* example:

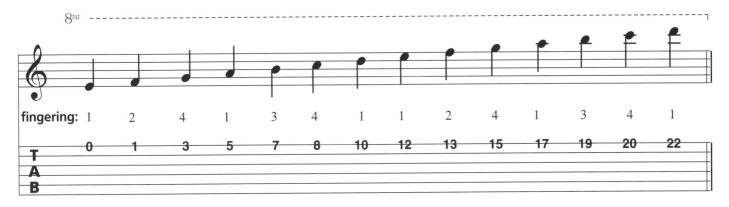

This can be thought of as three notes from the open *E Phrygian* pattern, three notes from the 5th fret *A Aeolian* pattern, one note from the 10th fret *D Dorian* pattern, and then repeat, starting with the 12th fret *E Phrygian* pattern. Other combinations of minor modes segments are, of course, also possible. This will also work using horizontal scales on the other strings.

Here is a table showing you the six horizontal scales for the *C major* family of modes (which includes *E Phrygian*.)

FRET NO.	0	1	2	3	4	5	6	7	8	9	10	11	12	13	14	15	16	17	18	19	20	21	22
String 1	E	F		G		A		B	C		D		E	F		G		A		B	C		D
String 2	B	C		D		E	F		G		A		B	C		D		E	F		G		A
String 3	G		A		B	C		D		E	F		G		A		B	C		D		E	F
String 4	D		E	F		G		A		B	C		D		E	F		G		A		B	
String 5	A		B	C		D		E	F		G		A		B	C		D		E	F		G
String 6	E	F		G		A		B	C		D		E	F		G		A		B	C		D

Afterword

You now have available to you a number of scales and theoretical concepts to help you use them. I'd like to make a few suggestions:

- Memorize all of the scale "shapes," and be able to play any of them starting in any position.

- Memorize the modal relationships for each key family. In other words, know all the relative modes for any given mode, in any key, anywhere on the fretboard.

- Derive and memorize all the horizontal scales for each mode in each key.

- Practice connecting the various modal "shapes" so that you can play smooth lines that cover the entire fretboard.

- When getting ready to play lead, analyze the chords of the music you will be playing. Be sure you know what key or keys it is in. If it changes keys, analyze the key changes, and find parallel modes that will allow you to make smooth transitions.

Most guitarists learn the vertical scales and become proficient with them. The horizontal scales, however, are frequently ignored or under-emphasized, yet they are extremely important to fretboard mastery. Don't forget them!!!

Finally, always remember that we all play music because it holds something very deep meaning for us. Don't let all the technical and theoretical information you acquire interfere with your enjoyment of the music — that enjoyment is, ultimately, the only thing that matters!

Have fun, and keep rockin'!!!

Michael